# Core Cutting Guide

**PAUL MITCHELL**®

**the school**

First published in the USA by W. Claybaugh
and PAUL MITCHELL THE SCHOOL
1534 Adams Avenue
Costa Mesa, California 92626-5375
(877) 903-5375
www.paulmitchelltheschool.com

ISBN # 0-9743205-2-8

Publishing: Winn Claybaugh
Editing: Susan Papageorgio, Inspired Learning LLC
Design: Jane Lacy, JSL Design LLC
ArtWork: SqueakStreet
Photography: Dave Schwep
Hair and Makeup: PAUL MITCHELL THE SCHOOL Advanced Academy Team

## Thank You
### Contributions and Acknowledgements

| | | | |
|---|---|---|---|
| Melinda Ashley | Douglas Christensen | Dennis James | Crystal Tesinsky |
| David Bangham | Scott Cole | Jason Jamiel | Jake Thompson |
| Vince Bough | Robert Cromeans | Jennifer Johnson | Shawn Trujillo |
| Cynthia Butler | Gregory Dunham | Angie Katsanevas | Candice Villarreal |
| Matthew Butler | Rosie Fuentes | Carolyn Nelson | Jodi Wonacott |
| Tommy Callahan | Jamie Griffith | Cindy Nelson | |
| Andrew Carruthers | Chris Halladay | Louis Orozco | |
| Kate Caussey | Michael Helm | Kazhal Showani | |

# Mission

## How we support our vision

When people come first,
success will follow.

# Table of Contents

## Introduction

One-Length

Graduated

Layered

# Introduction

## Why

Haircutting is a craft that requires consistent practice and patience to perfect your skill and artistry. PAUL MITCHELL THE SCHOOL Core Cutting System was developed with the serious craftsperson in mind. The learning system was designed to help you establish a solid foundation in the core fundamental haircutting skills. As you master these core skills you will be able to easily create basic, classic, and trend looks on a variety of clients and models.

## What

PAUL MITCHELL THE SCHOOL Core Cutting System utilizes the same principles of design that are used by some of the industry's most skilled artisans. At the root of the Core Cutting System are the 3 Principles of Dimension, which include height, width, and depth. These basic principles act as a blueprint that simplifies the design process.

The Core haircuts are divided into nine straightforward exercises that integrate round, square, and triangular geometries with the classic one-length, graduated, and layered cutting techniques. You will learn how to apply the 3 Principles of Dimension, the geometries, and techniques toward developing and expanding your haircutting skills.

This interactive learning system includes:
**PAUL MITCHELL THE SCHOOL Core Cutting Guide** – a learning guide with detailed simple technical explanations and step-by-step procedures for the nine Core haircut exercises.

**PAUL MITCHELL THE SCHOOL Core Cutting DVD System** – a visually stimulating 3-DVD set learning library; organized by one-length, graduated, and layered techniques.

**PAUL MITCHELL THE SCHOOL Diagramming System** – a unique, visual haircut-mapping tool.

**PAUL MITCHELL THE SCHOOL Core Cutting Skill Cards and PAUL MITCHELL Product Recipe Cards** – two essential quick reference tools that highlight the key points to remember and essential product recipes for creating and maintaining the looks featured in the Core Cutting System.

# How

Start by previewing this guide, which is divided into five key areas of learning to include:

| | | |
|---|---|---|
| **Chapter 1** | The Facts | The factors that affect the haircut. The basic principles behind haircutting design. |
| **Chapter 2** | The Words | The terminology and professional language needed to master the craft. |
| **Chapter 3** | The Tools | The tools and logistics needed to successfully perform haircutting services. |
| **Chapter 4** | The Method | The step-by-step process for each haircut exercise, including detailed diagrams and key points to remember. |
| **Additional Information** | | Additional logistical checklists and terminology. |

Preview The Core Cutting DVD program, which outlines each haircut exercise. The DVD program features multiple camera perspectives, freeze frame viewing, and an easy to navigate system of menus. Familiarize yourself with the DVD program, then choose one of the haircut exercises to practice.

As you view the DVD program, following along in this guide, take notes and diagram the haircut exercises. Practice what you learned on a mannequin or live model. Finally, use the Core Cutting Skills Cards as a quick reference in the salon or on the clinic floor.

To master all nine exercises, focus on each exercise until you feel you can perform the steps effectively. You may want to continue your learning by attending a PAUL MITCHELL ADVANCED ACADEMY Course to further develop your technical skills.

Core cutting skills will help you to build a skill foundation that will help you to master your craft and develop your technical artistry. When you first understand the "why's" and the "what's" of haircutting the "how" naturally follows.

# Chapter 1

## The Facts

- **The 3 Principles of Dimension**
- **Technique**
- **Geometry**
- **Section Angle Accuracy**
- **Hand and Body Position**
- **Hand Position Guidelines**
- **Tension**
- **Phases of a Shape**
- **Bone Structure of the Skull**
- **Top 10 Tips**

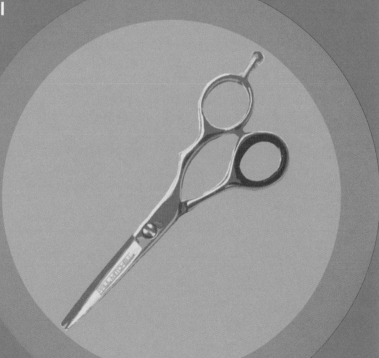

PAUL MITCHELL.
**the school**

# The 3 Principles of Dimension

Successful craftspersons and artists have the ability to visualize their completed work prior to starting the design and creation process. They think three dimensionally, meaning they use the design principles of height, width, and depth to create three-dimensional shapes and structures.

PAUL MITCHELL THE SCHOOL Core Cutting System uses the same artistic and design principles. The system suggests that you expand your perception by using a concept we call the 3 Principles of Dimension.

Dimension simply means to measure and define. The 3 Principles of Dimension include defining the height, width, and depth of an overall haircut shape. The 3 Principles of Dimension are used to help predetermine the desired end shape or architecture of a haircut.

The 3 Principles of Dimension are like a blueprint, guiding the architectural design of your work. You will use these principles when choosing the technique, elevation, geometry, and sectioning of your haircuts. These simple principles are the details you will need to expand your awareness and to consciously design three-dimensional shapes.

Successful haircutting designs are created with patience and attention to detail.

**Height**    Height is the vertical characteristics of a shape. It is the measurement of a shape, up and down.

Height is defined by the technique. The three techniques include one-length, graduated, and layered.

Technique describes how weight within a haircut is distributed vertically. Technique is created and controlled by the elevation of a hair section while cutting.

Elevation is the degree you lift the section of the hair, up or down.

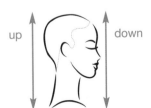

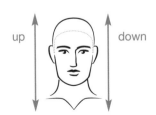

# The 3 Principles of Dimension

**Width**
Width in haircutting is the horizontal characteristic of the shape. It is the measurement of a shape from side to side. The width of a shape describes how the weight is distributed around the head.

- Width relates to geometry.
- Geometry is the amount of density distributed horizontally in a haircut.
- There are three basic geometries within the Core Cutting System, including square, round, and triangular.
- The geometry is controlled by the overdirection of the hair section while cutting.
- Overdirection is the degree that a section of hair is directed from side to side.

"Depth in haircutting is the measurement of distance the hair extends from the skull."

**Depth**
Depth in haircutting is the measurement of distance the hair extends from the skull. Depth is also known as the length of the haircut.

- Depth is determined by a combination of factors including hair texture, hair density, hair quality, and hair condition.
- Depth is the length of the hair on which the technique and the geometry are executed.
- The length or depth of the hair often depends on your client's preference.

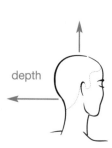
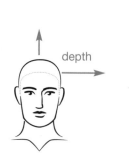
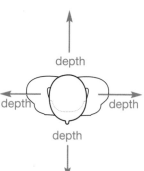

# The 3 Principles of Dimension

"Depth is the length that is ultimately created by the technique and geometry used."

## Hair Texture and Density

| | |
|---|---|
| **Fine Hair** | Fine hair responds best to haircut shapes that are above the shoulders. The longer the length of fine textured hair, the more thin or limp the hair appears. |
| **Medium Hair** | Medium texture and density hair is the most versatile and may be worn at any length. |
| **Thick Hair** | Thick or strongly textured hair becomes more solid and has less movement the shorter it is cut. |

## Hair Quality and Condition

Hair responds best to a haircut when it is in good quality and condition. Removing damaged hair helps to build a beautiful shape.

## Client's Desire

Many clients are very sensitive to the length of their hair. It is important to educate your clients about the best length for their hair.

# Technique

*Technique* describes how the weight is distributed vertically in a haircut shape. *Technique* is created by elevating the hair up or down. There are three *techniques,* including: *one-length, graduated,* and *layered.*

# Technique

**One-Length**  The *one-length technique* is cutting with 0-degree elevation. Hair is cut where it naturally falls.
The *one-length technique* creates maximum density.

*"The one-length technique is performed by cutting with 0-degree elevation."*

**Graduated**  The *graduated technique* is performed by elevating the hair section in a degree range of 1 to 89 while cutting.

The *graduated technique* builds weight away from the head shape.

The lower the *elevation* the heavier the *weight* buildup.
The higher the *elevation* the lighter the *weight* buildup.

*"The graduated technique is achieved by holding the hair section at a 1 to 89-degree range while cutting."*

**Layered**  The *layered technique* is achieved by holding the hair section at a 90-degree or higher elevation while cutting.

- The layered *technique* reduces weight within the shape.

- The higher the hair section is elevated while cutting, the lighter the layers will fall and appear.

*"The layered technique is achieved by elevating the hair section 90 degrees or higher while cutting."*

# Geometry

The *geometry* of a haircut is how *weight* is distributed horizontally within a shape. *Geometry* is created by directing the hair section backward or forward.

There are three *geometries: square, round, and triangular.*

**Round**    Round *geometry* is created by overdirecting the hair forward.

- Forward *overdirection* makes the hair progressively longer toward the back.
- Round *geometry* helps to push the hair away from the face.

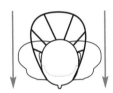

Round

**Square**    Square *geometry* is a strong linear shape that is created by a combination of overdirecting the hair section forward and backward to create a square, producing corners at the round of the head.

- Square *geometry* is used to create versatile movement forward and backward.

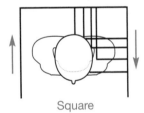

Square

**Triangular**   *Triangular geometry* is created by overdirecting hair back away from the face.

- *Triangular geometry* is used to push hair forward or toward the face to create an edgier look.

Triangular

**G E O M E T R Y**

Square

Round

Triangular

## Square One-Length

- Create four standard segments with a natural part.
- Start at the nape.
- Use one-inch horizontal sections that are parallel to the floor.
- Use no tension or overdirection, and use 0-degree elevation.
- Stand in a position that is consistent with square geometry.
- Comb hair to the natural fall.
- Cut the hair center to the left. Next cut the hair center to the right, using the backhand cutting method.
- Use the wide teeth of the comb to control the hair while cutting.
- Use the tension release method while cutting around the ear.
- Always use section angle accuracy.
- If you are left-handed, begin creating the basic shape on the opposite side of the head.

## Round One-Length

- Create four standard segments with a natural part.
- Start at the front temple area of the hairline.
- Use no tension or overdirection and use 0-degree elevation.
- Use horizontal-diagonal-back sections.
- Stand in a position that is consistent with round geometry.
- Cut inside the comb using the wide teeth to secure the hair section.
- Cut both sides of the hair prior to moving to the back sections to create balance.
- Use the tension release method while cutting around the ear.
- Continue to cut, using horizontal-diagonal-back sections through the back segment.
- Continue cutting through the back segments until you reach the natural fall.
- Cut the hair parallel to the section.
- Always use section angle accuracy.

## Triangular One-Length

- Create four standard segments with a natural part.
- Start at the back and center of the head.
- Use no tension or overdirection, and use 0-degree elevation.
- Use horizontal-diagonal-forward sections.
- Cut the hair working from the center to the left, using a normal cutting position.
- Next, cut the hair working from the center to the right using a backward cutting position.
- Stand in a position that is consistent with triangular geometry.
- Cut in comb, using the wide teeth of the comb to control the hair section.
- Use the tension release method when cutting around the ear.
- Continue to cut the hair until the natural fall is reached.
- Cut parallel to the section.
- Always use section angle accuracy.

## Square Graduation

- Create four standard segments with a natural part.
- Start in the back and center of the head.
- Create panels inside each standard segment.
- Take vertical-diagonal sections when cutting the back panels.
- Cut the hair using 45-degree elevation.
- Stand in a position that is consistent with square geometry.
- Overdirect the hair to the previously cut section.
- At the sides, use horizontal sections, starting at the mastoid process.
- Continue to cut the hair at a 45-degree angle, square to the head, and at a right angle.
- Always use section angle accuracy.

## Round Graduation

- Create four standard segments.
- Start in the front.
- Section the hair using horizontal-diagonal-back sections.
- Cut the hair sections using a 45-degree elevation.
- Stand in a position that is consistent with round geometry.
- Overdirect the hair slightly forward and onto the previously cut section.
- Continue to cut the hair until you reach the natural fall.
- At the sides, cut the hair using vertical-diagonal-back sections, behind the ear.
- The sections become horizontal-diagonal-back as you continue to cut, moving the hair up the head shape.
- Cut the hair at a 45-degree angle and parallel to the section.
- The cutting sections will cross over the back division line.
- Continue until you reach the natural fall.
- Always use section angle accuracy.

## Triangular Graduation

- Create four standard segments with a natural part.
- Start in the back.
- Section the hair using vertical-diagonal-forward sections.
- The sections will rotate from vertical-diagonal sectioning to horizontal-diagonal-forward sectioning.
- Cut the hair using a 45-degree elevation.
- Stand in a position that is consistent with triangular geometry.
- Overdirect the hair back onto the previously cut section.
- At the sides, from the high occipital area to the top of the ear, cut the hair parallel to the section.
- Decrease section elevation at the ear and continue to overdirect the hair back while cutting.
- Always use section angle accuracy.

## Square Layers

- Create four standard segments with a center part.
- Overdirect the hair sections straight and cut the sections square.
- Overdirection is strongest in the parietal ridge area.
- Continue to cut using vertical sectioning.
- Stand in a position that is consistent with square geometry.
- Comb sections flat from the scalp and square to the ceiling.
- At the sides, take vertical sections from the parietal ridge toward the hairline.
- Continue to comb each section straight out, holding the section square from the head.
- Always use section angle accuracy.

## Round Layers

- Create four standard segments with a center part.
- Start the haircut in the front; take vertical sections from the apex working toward the front hairline.
- Elevate the hair 90-degrees from the round of the head.
- Overdirect the hair section back onto the previously cut section.
- Use wagon wheel sectioning and continue cutting to the back.
- Stand in a position that is consistent with round geometry.
- Always use section angle accuracy.

## Triangular Layers

- Create four standard segments with a center part.
- Start the cut in the back of the head.
- Create a panel in each segment from the high occipital area to the top of the ear.
- Cut in a flat line, from the floor to the ceiling and parallel to the wall.
- Elevate the hair 90-degrees, starting in the center and working left.
- Use vertical cutting sections.
- Cut the hair square and flat to the head.
- Create a panel in each section at the low crown.
- Stand in a position that is consistent with triangular geometry.
- Continue cutting into the side segments taking horizontal-diagonal-forward sections from the crown to the temple area.
- Use a traveling guide until you reach the back of the ear.
- At the ear area, the guide becomes stationary.
- Use horizontal sections on the top of the head.
- Always use section angle accuracy.

# Section Angle Accuracy

Sectioning the hair is key to controlling the outcome of the haircut.
Proper and clean sectioning helps to keep your haircut on track.
A section is like a road map to reach your ultimate destination.

Choose the appropriate section angle to achieve the desired technique.
The key to choosing the section angle is determined by the technique
(one-length, graduated, layered) used. Sections should be parallel to
the cutting line.

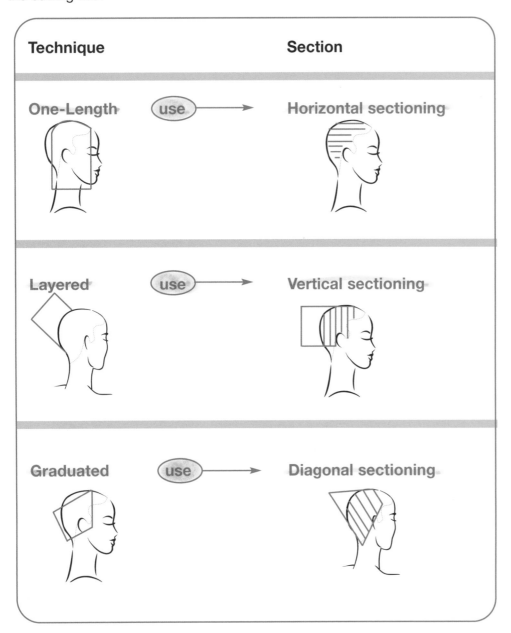

| Technique | | Section |
|---|---|---|
| One-Length | use → | Horizontal sectioning |
| Layered | use → | Vertical sectioning |
| Graduated | use → | Diagonal sectioning |

# Section Angle Accuracy

Section angles may be combined to create diversity.
See the examples below.

Combine horizontal and diagonal sections to create low graduation:

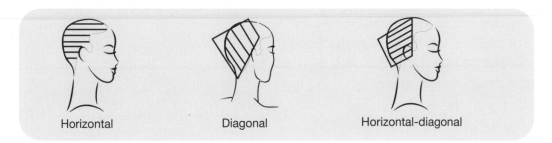

Horizontal          Diagonal          Horizontal-diagonal

Combine vertical and diagonal sectioning for high and flatter graduation:

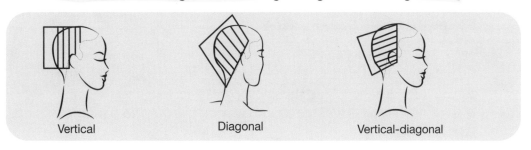

Vertical          Diagonal          Vertical-diagonal

# Sectioning Is Like a Road Map

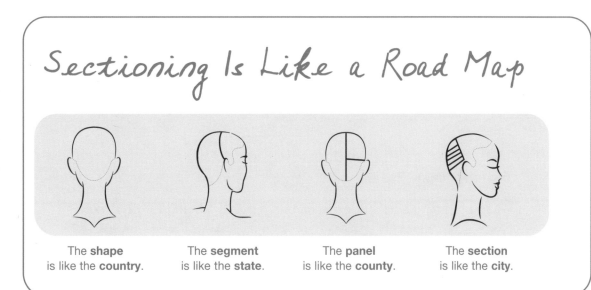

The **shape** is like the **country**.

The **segment** is like the **state**.

The **panel** is like the **county**.

The **section** is like the **city**.

# Hand and Body Position

Controlled haircutting is achieved by properly sectioning the hair and by using proper hand and body positions. Think of your body as a crane; the upper body lifts and the lower portion of your body controls overall movement and position. The position of your feet, your body, and your hands help to create the final haircut.

**Lower Body and Foot Position**

The lower body controls the geometric shape of the hair, which includes *round*, *square*, or *triangular*. Be conscious of the position of your feet and hips. They control the geometric shape.

Each haircut may be choreographed by standing in the shape you desire to cut. Your position helps to make overdirection feel more natural.

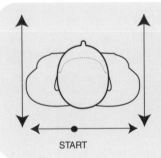

### Square Geometry Body Position

When executing a haircut exercise that requires a square geometric shape, position your body around your client forming a square. When cutting the sides, your hips should be parallel to your client's side. When cutting the back of the shape, your hips should be parallel to your client's back.

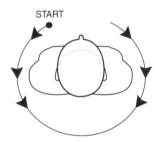

### Round Geometry Body Position

When executing a haircut exercise that requires a round geometric shape make sure that you position your body in a circle around your client as you cut the hair.

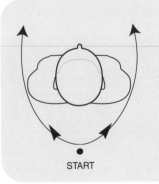

### Triangular Body Position

When executing a haircut exercise that requires a triangular geometric shape, form a triangle around your client as you cut the hair. A triangular body position is achieved by starting at a center point in the back and working toward the right. Lead with your right leg, pointing your right foot forward as you work toward the front. When working on the left side, turn to a center point in the back and lead with your left leg, pointing your left foot forward as you work toward the front.

# Hand and Body Positions

| Cutting | Technique | Tension |
|---|---|---|
| Cutting in comb | One-length | No tension |
| Cutting inside hand | Graduated | Medium tension |
| Cutting overhand | Layered | Maximum tension |

# Hand Position Guidelines

**Upper Body**

The upper body controls the technique, which includes *one-length*, *graduated,* or *layered*. The position of your elbows and shoulders should be parallel to the cutting section.

- Position your shoulders and elbows parallel to the cutting section.
- Proper shoulder positioning helps you to properly elevate the hair.

**Hands**

The way the hair is held within the hands will significantly affect the haircut. The proper hand position and finger tension should be chosen to support the desired technique.

- Cutting inside the hand gives medium tension and is best for creating graduation.
- Cutting outside the hand gives maximum tension and is best for layered haircuts.

**Cutting In Comb**

When cutting "in comb," the tip of the scissors should be going in the same direction when cutting on both sides of the head, which means you will have to cut backhanded on one side.

**Cutting Inside the Hand**

When cutting inside the hand, your index finger should lead or point the way.

**Cutting Overhand**

When cutting overhand, the pinkie should lead or point the way.

# Tension

Tension is created by the hand position.

## No Tension

No tension is created when the hair section is controlled inside of the comb. This allows hair to fall freely into gravity. No tension keeps the position of the hair section at its lowest elevation.

## Medium Tension

Medium tension is created by controlling the hair section between the index finger and the middle finger with the palm facing out.

## Maximum Tension (The Most Tension)

The most tension is created by controlling the hair section between the index finger and the middle finger, palm down, also known as the overhand position.

# Phases of a Shape

All haircuts have four design or execution phases. Great haircuts are achieved through disciplined cutting and styling in all four phases.

## Phase 1

### Creating the Basic Shape

When you create the basic shape, you are creating the overall framework. The basic shape should be performed wet for best control and precision.

**THE BASIC SHAPE = *Technique + Geometry + Depth***

## Phase 2

### Cross Checking

Cross checking is an "inspection" process, which ensures balance and precision. Use sections opposite to the original sections, being careful to follow the same geometric pattern while checking. Hold hair at the same elevation and overdirection angle as the original haircut sections.

- Cross check vertically to balance the technique.
- Cross check horizontally to balance the geometry.

During the cross checking phase inspect and evaluate your work. Determine what is working and change what is not working.

**CROSS CHECKING = Inspecting the shape.**

# Phases of a Shape

## Phase 3

### Blow Dry

There are three steps to the blow dry phase including step one, *flat-wrapping,* step two, *leafing*, and step three, *beveling*.

**A. Flat-wrapping**

Blow dry hair forward or backward to remove about 80% of the moisture from the hair.

**B. Leafing**

To finish the blow dry use the same sections that were used during the haircut.

**C. Beveling**

Beveling is performed as the final step of the blow dry on one-length haircut shapes.
Beveling creates a consistent direction at the ends of the hair.

**BLOW DRY = Preparation for refinement.**

## Phase 4

### Refinement

After the blow dry, visually check the hair and refine the shape.

**REFINEMENT = Detailing and personalizing.**

# Bone Structure of the Skull

The bone structure of the skull affects the overall shape of the haircut. The shape and contour of the head affects hair growth patterns and how the hair responds to being cut. Each area of the skull can be used as a reference point during the cutting process.

You can use these points and areas to guide how you approach your haircut. By being aware of the structure of the skull you can make conscious decisions about the sectioning, tension, elevation, direction, or overdirection you use when creating a balanced and beautiful shape.

*"Start a haircut at the shortest point."*

## Parts of the Skull

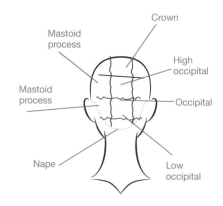

| | |
|---|---|
| **Apex** | The apex is the highest point at the top of the skull and is located by placing the comb on the top of the head. The comb will rest on this point. |
| **Crown** | The crown is the area on the skull that is between the apex and the back of the parietal ridge. The crown may be a flat area of the skull. |
| **Frontal** | The frontal area is the part of the skull located front and center, directly above the forehead. |
| **Mastoid Process** | The mastoid process is located in the back of the skull, directly behind both ears. The mastoid process starts at the high occipital and continues on to the side of the nape. |

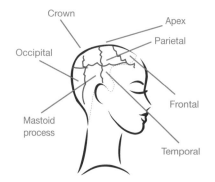

| Occipital Bone | The occipital bone is a protruding bone in the back of the head, found by placing a comb at the nape. The bone is found where the comb leaves the head. |
|---|---|
| Parietal Ridge | The widest area of the head starting at the temples and ending at the bottom of the crown. The parietal ridge is the point where the head begins to curve away from the comb, when the comb is placed flat at the side of the head. |
| Temporal | The temporal area is the part of the skull that starts at the front just before the hairline begins to recede and continues on directly behind the upper tip of the ear. |

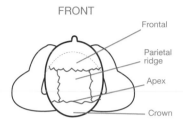

FRONT
Frontal
Parietal ridge
Apex
Crown

# TOP 10 TIPS FOR
# HAIRCUTTING

1. The higher you lift the hair the lighter the hair will be.

2. Short hair always directs longer hair.

3. Start a hair cut at the shortest point.

4. The lower body affects the desired geometry.

5. The upper body affects the desired technique.

6. Section angles affect the technique.
   One-length = horizontal section angles
   Graduated = diagonal section angles
   Layered = vertical section angles

7. When using an inside hand position, allow the index finger to lead the way. When using an overhand position allow the pinkie to lead the way.

8. One-length hair is created by using no tension and 0-degree elevation. Graduation is created by using medium tension and 1 to 89-degree elevation. Layered hair is created with maximum tension, and 90 degree or higher elevation.

9. Stay disciplined and controlled during all four phases of the haircut: the basic shape phase, cross checking phase, blow drying phase, and refinement phase.

10. Blow dry hair with the same sections and elevation that you cut with.

# Chapter 2

## The Words

- **Parts of the Head and Hair**
- **Geometry**
- **General Techniques**
- **Positions**
- **Controls**
- **General Terminology**
- **Cutting Terminology**
- **Standard Segmenting Terminology**

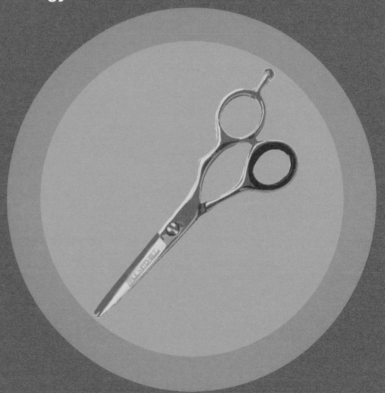

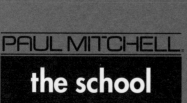

# The Words

The craft of hairdressing is filled with technical terms and words that make up a unique professional language. It is important to learn the terminology used in the Core Cutting System because the words graphically direct you toward the proper procedure. You will want to use these words when working with other professionals, and when using technical terminology with clients, you will always want to clearly define the words you are using.

The terminology in this chapter is a preview and a review of words you may be or have been exposed to during the learning process. The words are divided into: parts of the head and skull, geometry, techniques, positions, controls, cutting terminology, standard segmenting, and general terminology. Understanding and speaking a consistent language will help you to learn faster and retain what you have learned longer.

*To learn these words you may want to create flash cards. Place the word on an index card and its corresponding definition on the back.*

## Parts of the Head

| | | |
|---|---|---|
| **Shape** | A haircut according to a predetermined plan. *Technique + Geometry + Distance* | The **Shape** is like the **Country**. |
| **Segment** | The head is divided into four working areas. | The **Segment** is like the **State**. |
| **Panel** | A smaller working area within the segment. | The **Panel** is like the **County**. |
| **Section** | The hair held within the fingers to be cut. | The **Section** is like the **City**. |

Planes within the shape are the horizontal, diagonal, and vertical lines found in the head. The planes are determined by the bone structure of the skull.

# Bone Structure of the Skull

The bone structure of the skull affects the overall shape of the haircut. The shape and contour of the head affect hair growth patterns and how the hair responds to being cut. Each area of the skull can be used as a reference point during the cutting process.

You can use these points and areas to guide how you approach your haircut. By being aware of the structure of the skull you can make conscious decisions about the sectioning, tension, elevation, direction, or overdirection you use when creating a balanced and beautiful shape.

## PARTS OF THE SKULL

| | |
|---|---|
| **Apex** | The apex is the highest point at the top of the skull and is located by placing the comb on the top of the head. The comb will rest on this point. |
| **Crown** | The crown is the area on the skull that is between the apex and the back of the parietal. The crown may be a flat area of the skull. |
| **Frontal** | The frontal area is the part of the skull located front and center, directly above the forehead. |
| **Mastoid Process** | The mastoid process is located in the back of the skull, directly behind both ears. The mastoid process starts at the high occipital and continues on to the side of the nape. |
| **Occipital Bone** | The occipital bone is a protruding bone in the back of the head, found by placing a comb at the nape. The bone is found where the comb leaves the head. |
| **Parietal Ridge** | The widest area of the head starting at the temples and ending at the bottom of the crown. The parietal ridge is the point where the head begins to curve away from the comb, when the comb is placed flat at the side of the head. |
| **Temporal** | The temporal area is the part of the skull that starts at the front just before the hairline begins to recede and continues on directly behind the upper tip of the ear. |

# GEOMETRY

The geometry refers to the aspects of a haircut, created by overdirection.

| | |
|---|---|
| **Geometric Shapes** | A recognizable shape that could be measured, diagrammed, or described, such as a square, circle, or triangle. |
| **Round Geometry** | Is characterized by a weight balance that falls shortest in front and longest in the back. Round geometry is created by overdirecting the hair forward and is used to push hair away from the face. |
| **Triangular Geometry** | Is characterized by a weight balance that is shorter in the back and longer in the front. Triangular geometry is created by overdirecting the hair back and is used to push hair toward the face. |
| **Square Geometry** | Is characterized by weight that is equally balanced in front and in back. Square geometry is created by using a combination of forward and backward overdirection. |

# TECHNIQUES

Techniques are the vertical characteristics of a haircut created by elevation.
There are three Core techniques, including:

| | |
|---|---|
| **One-Length** | Refers to the maximum density within a haircut's shape, created by cutting the hair at 0-degree elevation. |
| **Graduated** | Refers to the building up of weight away from the head shape, characterized by a shorter length of hair at the bottom of the head shape and building to longer length at the top of the head. Graduation is created by cutting the hair in a range from 1 to 89-degrees. |
| **Layered** | Refers to a method for removing weight in a specific area, using 90-degree elevation or higher. The higher the elevation, the more weight is reduced. Layered hair is characterized by shorter lengths at the top of the head than at the bottom. |

# POSITIONS

Refers to the position of the client, stylist or the stylist's scissors.

| | |
|---|---|
| **Client Head Position** | The best position for the client's head while cutting is in a natural position. |
| **Body Position** | Refers to the position of the upper and lower body of the stylist. The stylist's lower body position affects the geometric shape of the haircut (round, square, or triangular) and the upper body controls the technique used (one-length, layered, or graduated). |
| **Stylist Arm Position** | Pertains to the stylist's hand and arm holding the hair. Proper arm position is parallel with the section angle and cutting line in use. |
| **Stylist Hand Position** | The hand position controls the tension of the section. Proper finger angles can affect the weight of the hair section. Proper stylist hand position is characterized by holding fingers parallel to the section angle and cutting line. Hair held inside the hand is generally held lower and can build weight. Hair held outside the fingers creates more tension and is easier to elevate and remove weight. |
| **Scissor Position** | Pertains to the direction the scissors are pointing. Controls the cutting angle. Scissor position should be parallel with the section angle and cutting line. |

# STANDARD SEGMENTING

Refers to the area of the skull where the haircut may be performed.

| | |
|---|---|
| **Natural Fall or Distribution Point** | The natural fall or distribution point refers to the natural distribution of hair at the front round of the head. The natural fall describes how hair naturally responds to gravity. |
| **High Point or Apex** | The highest point on the head, determined when the head is in a natural upright position. The apex may be located by placing a comb on the top center of the head. |
| **Crown** | The back portion of the parietal bone, slightly below the apex area. |
| **Division Line** | A division line separates the front segment of the hair from the back segment of the hair. The division line is considered the "breaking" point of the planes and may be determined by parting the hair from the apex to the indentation behind the ear. |

# CONTROLS

Refers to the terminology used to control and direct the hair while cutting.

| | |
|---|---|
| **Depth** | Describes the length of the hair. Depth is affected by hair texture, density, condition, and quality. |
| **Outline** | Hair lengths that form a cutting guide around the hairline and form the outline of a style. |
| **Section Angle Accuracy** | The parallel section or parting made to the hair you are cutting. There are three section angles, including:<br>• Horizontal – creating maximum density<br>• Diagonal – builds weight<br>• Vertical – removes weight |
| **Tension** | Tension refers to the amount of pressure used when holding the hair. The tension affects the degree the hair stretches. Proper tension can be achieved when cutting up to the second knuckle, or when controlling the hair section in the comb. |
| **Overdirection** | Overdirection is the degree you move the hair from side to side, to create shorter to longer lengths. Overdirection creates the primary geometric shapes. |
| **Elevation** | Elevation is the degree the hair is lifted from its natural fall position. Elevation creates one-length, graduated, and layered techniques. |
| **Target or Guideline** | The cutting line or target used as a reference point to create a design. |

# CUTTING TERMINOLOGY

Refers to the terminology used to describe cutting procedures.

| | |
|---|---|
| **Palm-to-Palm Cutting** | The main hand position used for graduation with horizontal and diagonal lines inside the fingers. The palm of the hand holding the scissors faces the palm of the hand holding the hair. |
| **Scissor Over Comb** | A controlled method of cutting, characterized by using the comb to elevate or lift the hair while cutting with scissors. |
| **Bracing** | A control method characterized by holding the hair section in the comb and the closed scissor blades. |
| **Palming** | A technique of holding the scissors within the hand, blades closed in natural position. |

# GENERAL TERMINOLOGY

Refers to general terms used to discuss the technical haircutting process.

| | |
|---|---|
| **Volume** | The mass or fullness of hair. |
| **Cross Check** | Verifying the accuracy of a haircut by inspecting sections of the hair parted and held opposite or perpendicular to how the section was cut. |
| **Fringe** | The region of hair that falls over the forehead. |
| **Nape** | Lower back area of the head and neck, under the occipital bone. |
| **Horizontal** | Parallel to the floor or the plane of the horizon. |
| **Stationary Guideline** | A guideline that hair sections are brought to and compared to before cutting. |
| **Moving / Traveling Guideline** | A portion of cut hair that becomes a guideline for the next section to be cut. |
| **Tension Release Method** | A method to equalize hair tension when working around the ear. The method includes holding the hair in the comb, and tapping underneath the section with the scissor blades closed, prior to cutting the hair section. |
| **Uniform** | Hair that is equal length around the entire head. A uniform haircut is also referred to as a "90-degree haircut." A haircut that is uniform to the shape of the head shape. |
| **Balance** | To visually achieve equal proportions of weight distribution in relation to the shape of the head. |
| **Recession Line** | The deepest point of the front hairline on the head shape. |
| **Blending** | Connecting two sections of a haircut that are separate and/or different. |

# Chapter 3

## The Tools

- **Cutting Tools**
- **Hairdressing Tools**
- **Station Setup**
- **Preparing for a Haircut Service**

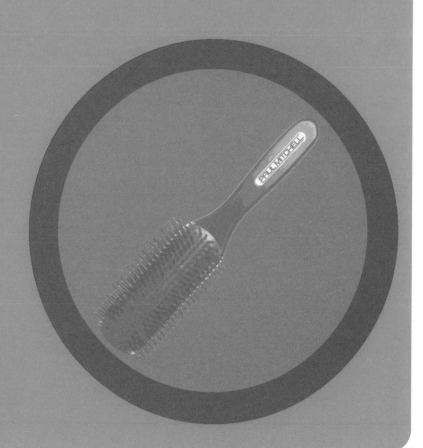

**PAUL MITCHELL**®
**the school**

# The Tools

Craftspersons are only as good as their tools. These are words to live by in an industry built on innovation and trends. You will want to invest a portion of your income each year in developing and maintaining your professional kit.

As a professional you must invest in and take care of your tools; your craft depends on it. In this chapter you will receive general recommendations and descriptions to guide you in building your kit.

## 4 Cool Tool Tips

There are four important things to remember about your tools:

1. **Build a relationship with a dependable vendor.** Choose reputable vendors who have excellent references and service histories.

2. **Shop at trade shows to learn more about what is available.** It is important to be aware of innovations. Research at trade shows and on line for the best tools for you.

3. **Learn how to take care of your tools.** Consistent and proper tool maintenance can add years to the life of your tools. Have your scissors sharpened by a reputable dealer.

4. **Buy what you like.** You can spend thousands of dollars on a variety of tools. When you buy what you like you will be more likely to use them.

Cutting Tools

<hr>

## SCISSOR LENGTHS

The length of your scissors determines the result.  Choose different size scissors for different jobs.

| | |
|---|---|
| **SMALL**<br>$4^{1/2} - 5^{1/2}$ inches | Used for graduated, short-layered haircuts, and detail work around the hair and neckline. |
| **MEDIUM**<br>6 inches | Your "workhorse" scissors, used for long, layered hair cutting and point cutting. |
| **LARGE**<br>$6^{1/2} - 7$ inches | Ideal for one-length lines, barbering, and scissor over comb techniques. |

<hr>

## SCISSOR TYPE

There are many different types of scissors ranging in quality and price. Scissors have become very specialized. It is important for you to determine what features you most prefer. The country of origin, type of metal, and blade style affect the quality and price.

| | |
|---|---|
| **Country of Origin** | Japan is known for manufacturing high quality scissors. |
| **Type of Metal** | The metal composition affects how clean the cut is and how long they stay sharp. Scissors are made from different metals, including stainless steel, cobalt alloy, titanium, and even ceramic! |
| **Length of Blade and Type of Blade** | Japanese manufactured scissors are known for their soft cut and clamshell edge.<br><br>German manufactured scissors are known for a hard cut and are primarily known to have serrated edges. |

# CHOOSING SCISSORS

There are many factors to consider when choosing scissors that are right for your needs.

| **Finger Holes and Hand Position** | Choose scissors that fit the size of hand. The wrong finger hole size may affect your ability to control the tool. Your ring finger and thumb should fit comfortably in the finger holes, going no deeper than the first knuckle, while your index and middle fingers should rest directly below the finger holes, but should not sit on the blades. |
|---|---|
| **Handle Features** | There are three different types of handles of scissors, including straight offset and extreme offset, which are called crane or gooseneck. Consider whether you need a tang or pinkie rest or purchase a scissor that has a removable rest. |
| **Tension** | Adjust the tension by using a small screwdriver or buy a scissor with a tension screw option. This allows you to loosen and tighten your implement, as you need to make adjustments. Be careful not to adjust the tension too tight or loose; this can ruin your scissors. |

# SPECIALTY SCISSORS

There are several different types of specialty scissors that help to create different effects and textures.

| **Texturing Scissors** | Notched blades remove bulk from hair in one stroke. Varieties differ in the number of teeth, starting at 5 notches and going up to 10, 15, 20, 30, and 40 notches. The more "teeth" or notches on the blades, the more bulk the scissors will remove. Invest in several to use on different textures of hair. |
|---|---|
| **Curved Scissors** | Curved blades are great for slicing, cutting curved lines, and cutting round or contoured shapes. They come in different sizes and shapes. |
| **Double or Triple Scissors** | Two or three pairs of scissors welded together. Used to chip and notch texture into the hair. This fun tool may be more impressive to your clients and interesting to other professionals, but is not a mandatory investment. |
| **Clippers** | Clippers are important for cutting short hair. Look for clippers that are sturdy and well balanced, not too top heavy or bottom heavy. A taper adjustment helps you to use the clipper in a variety of ways. Some clippers are manufactured with removable heads for flexibility in tapering. |
| **Razors or Carving Combs** | Razors and carving combs can help add fluidity and detail to your work Razors provide a slightly different and softer texture than other tools. |

# Hairdressing Tools

Let's learn how brushes are made and why it is important to choose the right brush for the right job.  By having a wide variety of brushes and combs and knowing how to use them, you can create trend and classic looks that your clients will love.

## COMBS

The right comb is critical to creating the desired result. Combs help control the hair with the right amount of tension.  The hair "fabric" responds differently when it is wet and when it is dry.

| | |
|---|---|
| **Wet Cutting Tools** | Wet hair responds well to smooth and supple, not rigid, combs. Combs made from rubber are best for cutting wet hair. |
| | **Suggestions include:**  *Beuy Pro Comb #101 and #105* – good for wet and precision haircutting. |
| **Dry Cutting Tools** | Cutting hair when it is dry creates refinement, meaning the hair will react in its own natural pattern as you comb through it. A carbon comb that is wider from the spine to the tips of the teeth with a matte finish works best. Matte finished combs grab the dry hair, making it easier to control. |
| | **Suggestions include:**  *Beuy Pro Comb #107*– good for dry cutting thick or coarse hair. |
| **Comb Colors** | Improve visibility by using lighter colored combs when cutting darker hair and dark combs when cutting lighter hair.  Use barbering combs when doing scissors over comb techniques and larger, wider-tooth combs for thick or coarse hair. |

# BRUSH SHAPES AND SIZES

Brushes help to control and style hair. Use the right brush for the right desired end result.

| | |
|---|---|
| **Round Brushes** | Round brushes provide lift and bend to the hair, working like a roller. The smaller the circumference of the brush, the tighter the curl or bend. Use smaller round brushes on shorter hair and larger brushes on longer hair. |
| **The Brush Core** | Some brushes have a metal or a ceramic core that holds heat, making it easier to bend and curl the hair shaft. |
| **Bristle Length** | The length of the bristles determines how deeply the brush will penetrate and grab the section. Long bristles will grab the hair and provide you with more control, while shorter bristles provide direction. |
| **Brush Styles:**<br><br>*Denman brushes*<br><br>*Flat brushes*<br><br>*Paddle brushes* | Have a variety of sizes and shapes, including flat and round brushes.<br><br>Flat brushes work best for a sleek finish. They provide a slight lift at the root area and a slight bend at the mid-shaft to the ends.<br><br>A paddle brush or a five-, seven-, or nine-row Denman brush is very good for a variety of styling needs. |

# CLIPS

Clips help control hair so that you may approach your work in a systematic way.

| | |
|---|---|
| **Duckbill Clips** | "Duckbill" clips are made from metal with a very strong spring; they last longer than plastic. They are used for fastening hair sections in place. |
| **Chignon Clips** | Chignon clips work well for long hair and dry cutting. |
| **Butterfly Clips** | Butterfly clips are used to keep your towels in place, not for securing the hair. |

# STYLING TOOLS

Your styling tools are another important part of your "tool box." You will need a quality blow dryer with nozzle, a variety of irons, and a diffuser to create a variety of finished looks.

| | |
|---|---|
| **Blow Dryers** | Blow dryers should have balanced construction. Test the balance by holding it in both hands and pointing the nozzle toward your chest, then away from your chest. Make sure it is comfortable to hold and not "back heavy." A nozzle directs the airflow to exactly where you want it and keeps the hair from blowing in every direction. Using the nozzle also helps to close the cuticle on the hair.<br><br>Temperature and air speed selections are very important. Low, medium, and high heat and airflow should be available, as well as a cold shot button. Make sure that buttons and switches are not in the way of your handgrip so that you will not inadvertently switch buttons on or off during styling. Check the cord. Make sure it is long enough and isn't likely to twist. |
| **Diffusers** | Diffusers attach to hair dryers and are used for styling curly hair. One with an "open basket" with "fingers" or prongs works well to define the curl. |
| **Irons** | Professional irons are very different than consumer irons. They are much hotter and usually do not have springs, so that you can better manipulate the heat across the hair shaft. The temperature control should range from 100 to 180 degrees. Start with metal irons and advance to irons with ceramic plates or wands. |
| **Round Iron** | Round irons provide curve and kink to the hair for a styled look. |
| **Flat Iron** | Flat irons create a linear and sleek look and can be used to tame overly curly hair.<br><br>A small, medium, and large set of both round and flat irons is recommended. A wet to dry flat iron is used on wet or damp hair. |

# The 5 Senses Program

By creating an environment and experience that appeals to your client's senses and preferences, you can attract and retain ideal clients. The 5 Senses Program is a guide for creating an unbelievable client experience.

*1* **Visual** – Clean up the mess! Clients love a clean place to come and relax. Your clients may have their car detailed often and employ a cleaning person. They may love to shop at Nordstrom's. Your goal is to create an environment that is cleaner than your client's home and as attractive as Nordstrom's. Arrange your tools and products in an appealing and organized manner. Decide which products you are using and which you want to promote for purchase.

Create interesting things for clients to look at. Hang current fashion images around the salon. Provide an updated stylebook, including pictures of your own work. Set out upbeat fashion, fitness, or health magazines.

Finally, look the part. One of the most important things you can do to appeal to your client's visual senses is to look the part of a successful image professional. They come to you for beauty and image advice and expect you to look the part.

*2* **Smell** – The sense of smell is strongly tied to memory. If you want your clients to remember you and their experience, use products with fragrances your client loves. If a client likes the way a product smells, it gives you an opportunity to point out the benefits of the products and encourage a purchase. When your client returns home and uses the products, she is likely to remember her great service experience. Think of hair care, skin care, and makeup products as a wonderful reminder for your client to return to you.

**The sweet smell of freshness** – Ensure good air quality in the school or salon.
- Remove offensive odors by misting the air, running an air purifier, or burning candles.
- Refrain from smoking between clients. Nonsmokers are especially sensitive to the smell of cigarettes.
- Make sure your breath is fresh and pleasant. Take a toothbrush and toothpaste to work and use mints.
- Wear a light fragrance. Use deodorant and make sure your clothes smell fresh.

**3** **Taste –** Do you offer refreshments to your clients? If so, great! What you serve is as important as how you serve it.

- Serve only fine quality coffee or teas, purified water, or any other drink that is refreshing and tasteful.
- Offer gourmet drinks in clean mugs and spot-free glasses. Avoid styrofoam.
- Serve lemonade or iced tea with real ice cubes and lemon wedges.
- Make sure the serving area is clean.
- Carry your clients' drinks back to your station for them.
- Offer refills and discard their glass or cup when they are finished.

**4** **Touch –** Client surveys have shown that what they liked best about their visit to the salon was the wonderful massage at the shampoo bowl. Invite your client to relax as you gently massage and release her tension and prepare her for an enjoyable service.

- During a shampoo, provide an extra long head massage.
- During a chemical service, surprise your client with a hand massage using a special lotion with her favorite fragrance.

**5** **Hearing –** Your clients' experience is profoundly shaped by what they hear. The music and conversation around them will put them in a state of relaxation or irritation. Clients will have a wide variety of musical tastes, but national surveys reveal that the majority of clients prefer light jazz music to any other. This means that you may have to endure listening to music that does not fit your taste. Remember that your role as a service provider is to provide a great experience for your client.

**Motivate yourself –** You can consistently meet your clients' needs by motivating yourself to do what your client loves, even if it isn't your most favorite thing to do.

To learn more about unbelievable customer service read *Connecting To My Future*, a PAUL MITCHELL THE SCHOOL PUBLICATION. Visit *www.paulmitchelltheschool.com* for more details.

"There are very few professions where touch is allowed. Take this unique opportunity to build a bond with your guest that may last for years."

# Learning Activity: Station Setup

- Make a list of what you need to successfully perform haircut services.
- Diagram your station setup.

## Station Setup

### Tools and Equipment

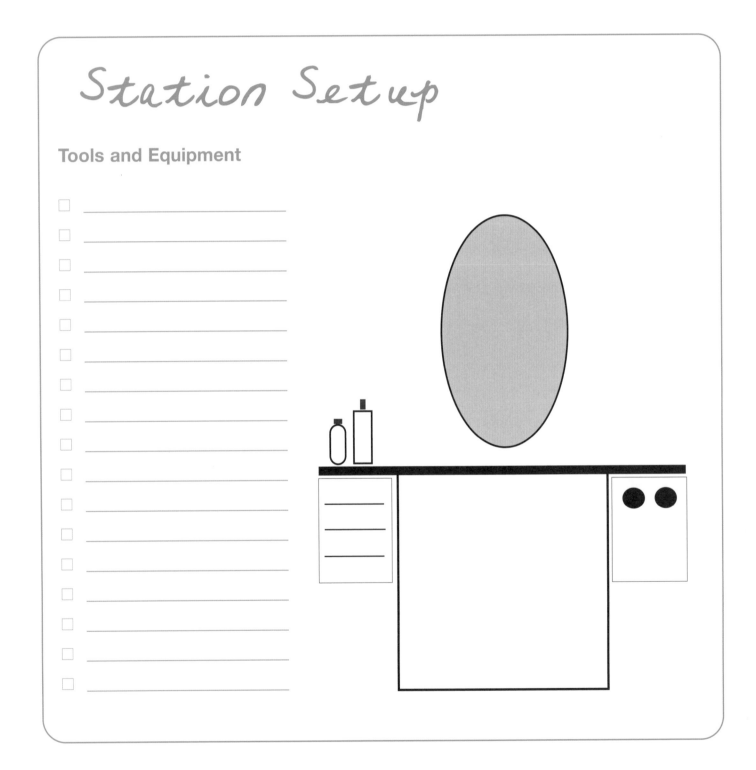

# Preparing for a Haircut Service

## To Do:
- Follow the 5 Senses Program.
- Sanitize your station.
- Wash hands with soap and water before and after each service.
- Prepare materials and supplies for the service.
- Place sanitized tools in a closed container or drawer.

## Cutting and Styling Tool Checklist:
Arrange your tools on your station, put in a clean sanitary container.
- Scissors
- Texture scissors
- Razor or carving comb
- Clippers
- Clips (wet and dry)
- Combs; for wet and dry cutting
- Brushes; flat brush, paddle brush, Denman brush
- Blow dryer, curling irons, and a flat iron

## Draping Materials:
Have draping materials at your station.
- Cape
- Neck strip
- Towel for shampooing

## Product Setup:
- Set up desired products: cleanse, condition, and styling products.
- Make sure the containers are clean of all product residue and hair.

## Additional Tips

- Always sanitize combs, brushes, scissors, clips, and other implements prior to use by washing thoroughly in soapy hot water.
- Replace blades in razors prior to each new client. Discard used blades in a puncture-proof container.
- Keep scissors in good working order by lubricating with the proper oil and wiping with a chamois (or dry cloth).
- Drape your guest properly for the shampoo and haircutting service.
- Follow the 10 Opportunities during the entire service.
- Complete the service using the 2-Minute Plan.

# Diagramming

Diagramming is an essential skill and is the most effective way of taking notes when learning a haircut or cutting method. Diagramming is also a great way of communicating your ideas with other professionals.

It is always a good idea to use colored pencils or pens when diagramming to help you distinguish your different lines and partings.

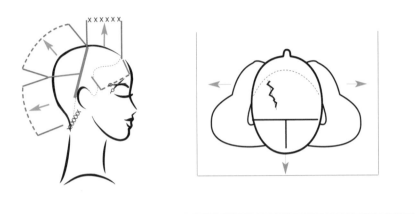

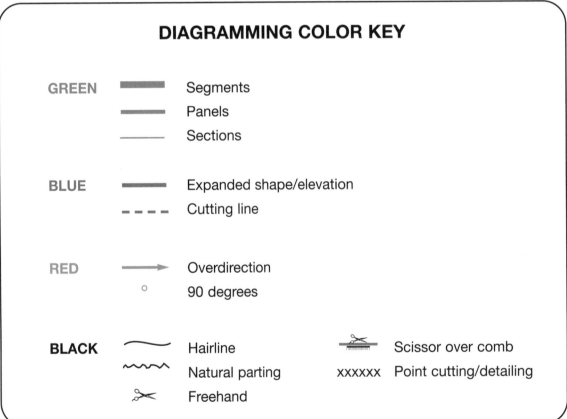

## DIAGRAMMING COLOR KEY

| GREEN | | |
|---|---|---|
| | ▬▬▬▬ | Segments |
| | ▭▭▭ | Panels |
| | ――― | Sections |

| BLUE | | |
|---|---|---|
| | ▬▬▬ | Expanded shape/elevation |
| | ─ ─ ─ ─ | Cutting line |

| RED | | |
|---|---|---|
| | ⟶ | Overdirection |
| | ○ | 90 degrees |

| BLACK | | | | |
|---|---|---|---|---|
| | ⌇ | Hairline | ✁ | Scissor over comb |
| | ⌇⌇⌇ | Natural parting | xxxxxx | Point cutting/detailing |
| | ✂ | Freehand | | |

Whenever diagramming you should always have a written note by each step to ensure at another time you or another professional will be able to interpret your drawings.

# Learning Activity: Diagramming

Go to the DVD program, review any haircut exercise, and try this new diagramming process.

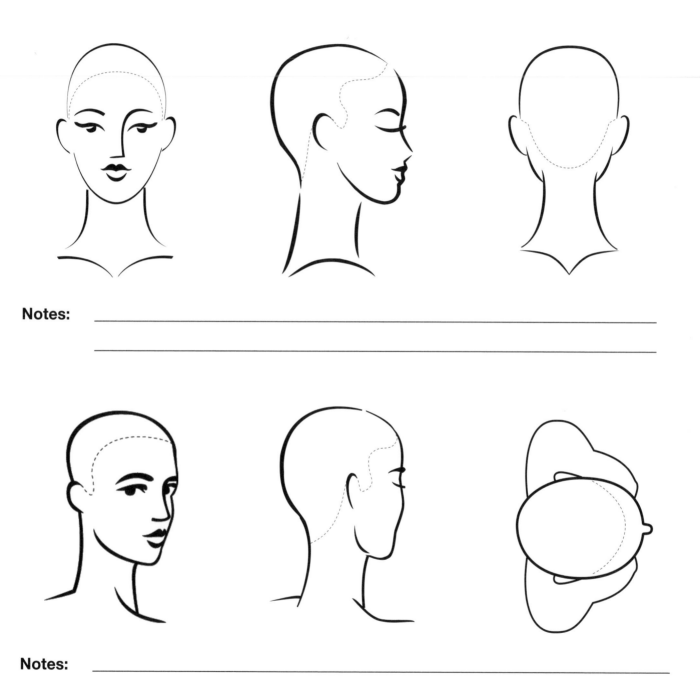

**Notes:** _____

_____

**Notes:** _____

_____

PAUL MITCHELL.
**PARTNER SCHOOL PROGRAM**

# Chapter 4

## The Method

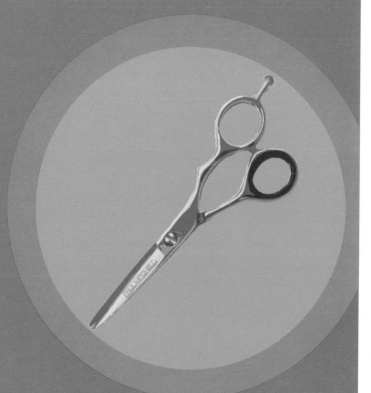

**PAUL MITCHELL**
**the school**

# Haircutting Guidelines

This chapter will focus on the step-by-step haircut exercises. It is important for you to be aware of the language and design principles that were the focus of previous chapters. You will notice that the haircut exercises include factors that affect the haircut. These factors help you to consciously manage and create the geometry, technique, elevation, overdirection, tension, section angle accuracy, and body positioning needed to create the final shape.

A good haircut is the result of consistent execution of these factors. Take a moment and test your knowledge:

## Your Core Cutting I.Q.

What are the 3 Principles of Design?

1. _____
2. _____
3. _____

What are the three section angles?

1. _____
2. _____
3. _____

What are the three Techniques?

1. _____
2. _____
3. _____

What are the three geometries within the Core Cutting System?

1. _____
2. _____
3. _____

What controls the technique? _____

Complete the following sentences:

1. Diagramming is like the _____.
2. The shape is like the _____.
3. The segment is like the _____.
4. The panel is like the _____.
5. The section is like the _____.

*Answers to the Core Cutting I.Q. Test are all located in the back of this guide.*

# Hand and Body Position

Preview the following nine haircutting exercises and determine the proper hand position, and upper and lower body position for each:

| HAIRCUT EXERCISE | HAND POSITION | UPPER BODY | LOWER BODY |
|---|---|---|---|
| Square One-Length | | | |
| Square Graduation | | | |
| Square Layers | | | |
| Round One-Length | | | |
| Round Graduation | | | |
| Round Layers | | | |
| Triangular One-Length | | | |
| Triangular Graduation | | | |
| Triangular Layers | | | |

# Success Guidelines

There are many important guidelines for proper haircutting. They should be followed closely to create a uniform haircut shape and design.

- Hair is always distributed into four working areas known as "segments."

- Always be aware of client's head position.

- Maintain your standing position throughout the cut to ensure consistency.

- Use equal tension when cutting hair. Tension changes when using a fine tooth comb versus a wide tooth comb.

- Do not set your comb down when cutting.

- Before each cut, find a visible guide through the sectioned off hair. If it cannot be found, reduce the size of the section.

- Do not cut past the second knuckle. If you cut between the second and third knuckle, the amount of tension changes, causing an uneven haircut.

- Always comb the section of hair to be cut, from the scalp to the guide.

- Hold the scissors at a consistent angle to the hair. The cutting line is parallel to the section.

- Neutral position or "palming" the scissors is done when combing or parting to make sure you don't mistakenly remove hair.

- The thumb controls the moving blade. The thumb is the only digit moving in order to create a consistent flowing line.

- The haircut exercises are divided into three techniques: one-length, graduated, and layered. The techniques are controlled by elevation.

- The techniques have three counterparts called geometries which include square, round, and triangular.

"Sadie"

 Square One-Length

 *Square One-Length*

## Haircut Description

The Square One-Length shape is described as having maximum density. The haircut is even in length from front to back.

## FACTORS THAT AFFECT THE HAIRCUT

| | |
|---|---|
| GEOMETRY | Square |
| TECHNIQUE | One-length |
| ELEVATION | None |
| OVERDIRECTION | None |
| TENSION | None |
| SECTION ANGLE ACCURACY | Horizontal |
| HAND POSITION | In comb |
| UPPER BODY | Horizontal |
| LOWER BODY | Square |

## *The Square One-Length Exercise*

### CREATING THE BASIC SHAPE

**STEP 1**   Create four standard segments with a natural part.

**STEP 2**   Start at the back nape. Take horizontal sections across both back segments the width of comb. Comb hair down to natural fall with wide teeth of the standard cutting comb. Use no tension, overdirection, or elevation.

**Your body position:** Stand in back of the client when cutting the back panels and stand at the side when cutting the sides.

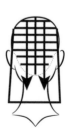

**STEP 3**    Comb hair down with the wide teeth of the comb, parallel to the parting and the floor. Continue taking horizontal sections, working from the center to the left, then center to the right, using backhand technique on second side. Continue to cut sections up the head. When cutting left-handed, start on the opposite segment.

**STEP 4**    When reaching the sections located above the ear, take the sections forward to the front hairline. When working around the ear, use the tension release method. Continue to cut each section until the natural fall is reached. When cutting the sides, stand at the side of your square. Keep arms, comb, and scissors parallel with the horizontal cutting section.

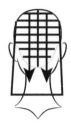

**CROSS CHECKING**    Cross checking a one-length shape is done by changing scissor direction.

**BLOW DRY**    **A.** Flat wrap hair by blow drying hair forward and backward to remove 80% of the moisture.

**B.** After most of the moisture has been removed, use a leafing technique using the same sectioning used for the cut. These methods are used to control hair and prepare it for refinement.

**C.** Direct and smooth the ends using the beveling blow dry procedure.

**REFINEMENT**    After the blow dry phase, visually check the haircut and refine the shape, customizing it to fit your guest's needs. Finish the service by completing the style, applying PAUL MITCHELL styling product, and using the 2-Minute Plan.

# Square One-Length Diagram

**Notes:** part naturally or dead center

— on right side, cut towards face

 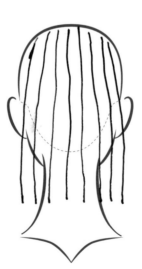 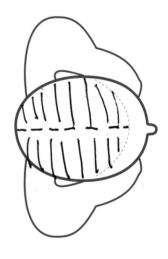

**Notes:** _____

_____

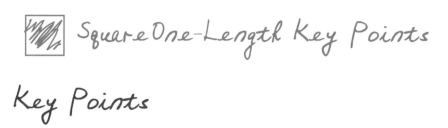 *Square One-Length Key Points*

# Key Points

### CREATING THE BASIC SHAPE

- Create four standard segments with a natural part.
- Start at the nape.
- Use one inch horizontal sections that are parallel to the floor.
- Use no tension, overdirection, and use 0-degree elevation.
- Stand in a position that is consistent with square geometry.
- Comb hair to the natural fall.
- Cut the hair center to the left. Next, cut the hair center to the right, using the backhand cutting method.
- Use the wide teeth of the comb to control the hair while cutting.
- Use the tension release method while cutting around the ear.
- Always use section angle accuracy.
- If you are left-handed, begin creating the basic shape on the opposite side of the head.

### CROSS CHECKING

- To cross check the basic shape, change scissor direction, keeping hair at 0-degree elevation.

### BLOW DRY

- **Flat wrap** – Blow dry the hair forward and backward to remove 80% of the moisture.
- **Leafing** – Blow dry the hair using the same sections used to create the basic shape.
- **Beveling** – Direct the airflow onto the ends while you roll the hair under with a paddle or Denman brush.

### REFINEMENT

- Visually check the haircut and refine the shape.
- Finish the service by applying PAUL MITCHELL finishing products.
- Complete the service using the 2-Minute Plan. Recommend the appropriate PAUL MITCHELL products.

*See Product Recipe Cards for product ideas.*

# Notes

"Shavonna"

Square Graduation

 *Square Graduation*

## Haircut Description

The Square Graduation haircut has a buildup of weight away from the skull. The back and front sections are connected by a corner at the mastoid process.

## FACTORS THAT AFFECT THE HAIRCUT

| | |
|---|---|
| GEOMETRY | Square |
| TECHNIQUE | Graduated |
| ELEVATION | 45-degrees |
| OVERDIRECTION | Backwards and forwards |
| TENSION | Medium |
| SECTION ANGLE ACCURACY | Vertical-diagonal-forward, and horizontal |
| HAND POSITION | Inside hand |
| UPPER BODY | Vertical-diagonal-forward, and horizontal |
| LOWER BODY | Square |

## The Square Graduation Exercise

### CREATING THE BASIC SHAPE

**STEP 1**    Create standard segments with a natural part. Create panels inside of those segments by making another division line horizontally at the top of the ears and at the crown.

**STEP 2**    Start in the center back at the bottom panel, taking vertical-diagonal-forward sections. Overdirect each section straight back to create a square.

**STEP 3**    Pull the hair straight back to the square and elevate, approximately 45-degrees. Remember, the higher the hair is elevated the lighter the graduation. Pay careful attention to the area behind the ear. Make sure that this section is overdirected straight back to maintain a square.

**STEP 4**   Cut both panels in the back segments, then cross check by using horizontal sections. Make sure to use the same elevation and overdirection you used while cutting.

**STEP 5**   Cut the third panel, starting at the crown and continuing to the apex area. Use vertical-diagonal-forward sections and maintain consistent elevation with both back panels.

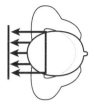

**STEP 6**   Continue to the side of the head, using horizontal sections that start at the mastoid process and continuing to the front hairline. A guide is obtained by taking previously cut sections at the mastoid process and swinging each section to a right angle.

**STEP 7**   Work with horizontal sections, using consistent elevation, cut the hair square and at a right angle to the back segments. Elevate each section slightly to the previous section as you work up toward the top of the head. Continue until you reach the natural fall.

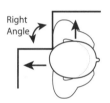

**CROSS CHECKING**   Cross check by using horizontal-diagonal-back sections to inspect the back segments and to check the sides. Remember to using the same elevation and overdirection that you used during the basic shape phase. Check for squareness.

**BLOW DRY**   **A.** Flat wrap hair by blow drying hair forward and backward to remove 80% of the moisture.

**B.** After most of the moisture has been removed, blow dry the hair, using the leafing technique with the same sectioning used for the cut. This method is intended to control hair and prepare it for refinement.

**REFINEMENT**   After the blow dry phase, visually check the haircut and refine the shape, customizing it to fit your guest's needs. Finish the service by completing the style, applying PAUL MITCHELL product, and completing the service using the 2-Minute Plan.

Square Graduation Diagram

 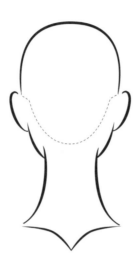 

**Notes:** _____

_____

 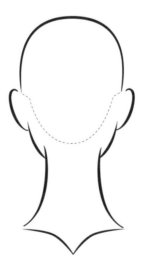 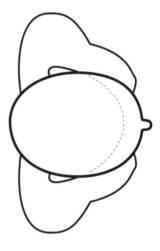

**Notes:** _____

_____

PAUL MITCHELL.
**the school**

 Square Graduation Key Points

## CREATING THE BASIC SHAPE

- Create four standard segments with a natural part.
- Start in the back and center of the head.
- Create panels inside each standard segment.
- Take vertical-diagonal sections while cutting the back panels.
- Cut the hair using 45-degree elevation.
- Stand in a position that is consistent with square geometry.
- Overdirect the hair to the previously cut section.
- At the sides, use horizontal sections, starting at the mastoid process.
- Continue to cut the hair at a 45-degree angle, square to the head, and at a right angle.
- Always use section angle accuracy.

## CROSS CHECKING

- To cross check the basic shape, use horizontal-diagonal-back sections, and vertical sections.

## BLOW DRY

- *Flat wrap* – Blow dry the hair forward and backward to remove 80% of the moisture.
- *Leafing* - Blow dry the hair using the same sections used to create the basic shape.

## REFINEMENT

- Visually check the haircut and refine the shape.
- Finish the service by applying PAUL MITCHELL finishing products.
- Complete the service using the 2-Minute Plan.
  Recommend the appropriate PAUL MITCHELL products.

*See Product Recipe Cards for product ideas.*

# Notes

PAUL MITCHELL
the school

"Kelly"

Square Layers

 *Square Layers*

## HAIRCUT DESCRIPTION

The Square Layers haircut includes layers cut in a balanced manner around the head shape with corners on the rounds of the head, producing volume and versatility.

## FACTORS THAT AFFECT THE HAIRCUT

| | |
|---|---|
| GEOMETRY | Square |
| TECHNIQUE | Layered |
| ELEVATION | 90-degrees |
| OVERDIRECTION | Backward and forward |
| TENSION | Maximum |
| SECTION ANGLE ACCURACY | Vertical |
| HAND POSITION | Overhand |
| UPPER BODY | Vertical |
| LOWER BODY | Square |

*The Square Layers Exercise*

### CREATING THE BASIC SHAPE

**STEP 1**    Create four standard segments, with a center part.

**STEP 2**    Start at the top center of the head segment. Take half inch sections from the apex to the front hairline. Overdirect the sections straight up and cut square to the ceiling.

Comb from the inside, between you and the section, as if you are combing from the top of a box.

The overdirection is the strongest in the parietal ridge area. Your elevation is straight up with a flat or square cutting line.

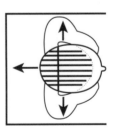

**STEP 3**   Continue to the apex and crown area, using the same cutting method, starting from the center. The cutting line should be continuous into the crown area.

**STEP 4**   Move to the side of the head, by taking a vertical section from the parietal ridge to the hairline, on the side of the head.

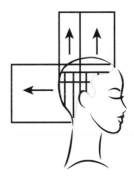

Each section is elevated 90-degrees and overdirected to a square plane, parallel with the wall.

A guide is obtained from the previously cut hair at the parietal ridge, swinging the hair section at a right angle.

Repeat steps on the opposite side of the head, working into the mastoid process area.

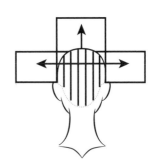

**STEP 5**   Move to the back segment. In the back maintain vertical sections. A guide is obtained by taking the previously cut hair at the crown.

Swing hair section at a right angle. Cut the back segments working from the center left to the right. Overdirect each section out to a flat plane in the back.

**CROSS CHECKING**   Cross check the entire shape using horizontal sections opposite to the original sections. Maintain the same overdirection and elevation.

**BLOW DRY**   **A.** Flat wrap hair by blow drying hair forward and backward to remove 80% of the moisture.

**B.** After most of the moisture has been removed use a leafing technique with the same sectioning used for the cut. These methods are intended to control hair and prepare it for refinement.

**REFINEMENT**   After the blow dry phase, visually check the haircut and refine the shape, customizing it to fit your guest's needs. Finish the service by completing the style, applying PAUL MITCHELL product, and using the 2-Minute Plan.

*Square Layers Diagram*

**Notes:** _____

_____

 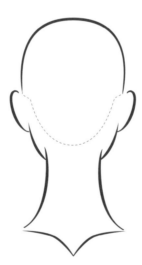 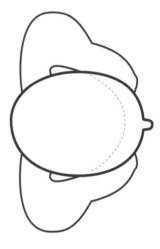

**Notes:** _____

_____

PAUL MITCHELL.
**the school**

## Square Layers Key Points

### CREATING THE BASIC SHAPE

- Create four standard segments with a center part.
- Overdirect the hair sections straight and cut the sections square.
- Overdirection is strongest in the parietal ridge area.
- Continue to cut using vertical sectioning.
- Stand in a position that is consistent with square geometry.
- Comb sections flat from the scalp and square to the ceiling.
- At the sides, take vertical sections from the parietal ridge, toward the hairline.
- Continue to comb each section straight out, holding the section square from the head.
- Always use section angle accuracy.

### CROSS CHECKING

- To cross check the basic shape use horizontal sections that are opposite to the original sections. Maintain the same overdirection and elevation that was used while creating the basic shape.

### BLOW DRY

- **Flat wrap** – Blow dry the hair forward and backward to remove 80% of the moisture.
- **Leafing** – Blow dry the hair using the same sections used to create the basic shape.

### REFINEMENT

- Visually check the haircut and refine the shape.
- Finish the service by applying PAUL MITCHELL finishing products.
- Complete the service using the 2-Minute Plan.
  Recommend the appropriate PAUL MITCHELL products.

*See Product Recipe Cards for product ideas.*

# Notes

 *Round One-Length*

## Haircut Description

The Round One-Length haircut is characterized by maximum density shape. It is shortest at the front hairline and progressively becomes longer toward the back.

## FACTORS THAT AFFECT THE HAIRCUT

| | |
|---|---|
| GEOMETRY | Round |
| TECHNIQUE | One-length |
| ELEVATION | None |
| OVERDIRECTION | None |
| TENSION | None |
| SECTION ANGLE ACCURACY | Horizontal-diagonal-back |
| HAND POSITION | Cutting in comb |
| UPPER BODY | Horizontal-diagonal-back |
| LOWER BODY | Round |

## *The Round One-Length Exercise*

### CREATING THE BASIC SHAPE

**STEP 1**     Create four standard segments, with a natural fall.

**STEP 2**     Start at the front temple areas of the hairline with horizontal diagonal back sections that extend back to the center back division line.

**STEP 3**     Comb hair down with the wide teeth of the comb, using no tension, overdirection, or elevation. Be cautious in the ear area. Use the tension release method. When cutting left-handed, start on opposite segment. Cut both sides, then check the balance.

**STEP 4**     Continue cutting sections, moving up the head, using consistent sectioning, combing, and no tension, until the "natural fall is reached."  Your arms, comb, and scissors are parallel to the sections.

**STEP 5**     Cut the opposite side of the hair using the same procedure and methods. Make sure to use the backhand method while cutting.

**CROSS CHECKING**     Cross checking a one-length shape is done by changing scissor direction.

**BLOW DRY**     **A.** Flat wrap hair by blow drying hair forward and backward to remove 80% of the moisture.

   **B.** After most of the moisture has been removed use a leafing technique with the same sectioning used for the cut. These methods are intended to control hair and prepare it for refinement.

   **C.** Direct and smooth the ends using the beveling blow dry procedure.

**REFINEMENT**     After the blow dry phase, visually check the haircut and refine the shape, customizing it to fit your guest's needs.  Finish the service by completing the style, applying PAUL MITCHELL product, and using the 2-Minute Plan.

# Round One-Length Diagram

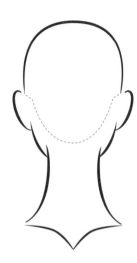

**Notes:** _____

_____

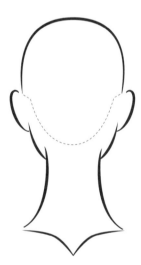
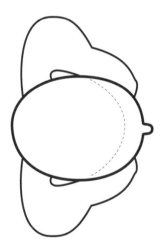

**Notes:** _____

_____

**PAUL MITCHELL**
**the school**

# Round One-Length Key Points

## CREATING THE BASIC SHAPE

- Create four standard segments with a natural part.
- Start at the front temple area of the hairline.
- Use no tension or overdirection, and use 0-degree elevation.
- Use horizontal-diagonal-back sections.
- Stand in a position that is consistent with round geometry.
- Cut inside the comb, using the wide teeth of the comb to control the hair section.
- Cut both sides of the haircut to create balance.
- Use the tension release method while cutting around the ear.
- Continue to cut, using horizontal-diagonal-back sections through the front and back segments.
- Continue cutting through the back segments until you reach the natural fall.
- Cut the hair parallel to the section.
- Always use section angle accuracy.

## CROSS CHECKING

- To cross check the basic shape, change scissor direction, keeping hair at 0-degree elevation.

## BLOW DRY

- *Flat wrap* - Blow dry the hair forward and backward to remove 80% of the moisture.
- *Leafing* - Blow dry the hair using the same sections used to create the basic shape.
- *Beveling* - Direct the airflow onto the ends, directing the ends down and under.

## REFINEMENT

- Visually check the haircut and refine the shape.
- Finish the service by applying PAUL MITCHELL finishing products.
- Complete the service using the 2-Minute Plan.
  Recommend the appropriate PAUL MITCHELL products.

*See Product Recipe Cards for product ideas.*

# Notes

PAUL MITCHELL
the school

"Jen Marie"

Round Graduation

 *Round Graduation*

## Haircut Description

The Round Graduation shape is described as having a buildup of weight away from the head. The shortest point of the haircut is at the front hairline. The hair becomes progressively longer toward the back.

## FACTORS THAT AFFECT THE HAIRCUT

| | |
|---|---|
| GEOMETRY | Round |
| TECHNIQUE | Graduated |
| ELEVATION | 45-degrees |
| OVERDIRECTION | Forward |
| TENSION | Medium |
| SECTION ANGLE ACCURACY | Vertical-diagonal-back at the mastoid process, pivoting to horizontal-diagonal-back sections at the occipital area. |
| HAND POSITION | Inside hand |
| UPPER BODY | Horizontal-diagonal-back at the temporal area, adjusting back to match section in the back. |
| LOWER BODY | Round |

*The Round Graduation Exercise*

## CREATING THE BASIC SHAPE

**STEP 1**       Create four standard segments with a natural part.

**STEP 2**       Start at the front with a horizontal-diagonal-back section from the front hairline to the division line behind the ear.

**STEP 3**   Stand in front of and forward of the segment; over-direct the hair forward. Elevate the hair 45-degrees from the base of each section to achieve the desired buildup of weight. The lower the elevation the heavier the graduation. When cutting left-handed, start on the opposite segment.

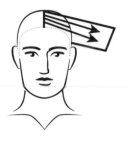

**STEP 4**   Each section is overdirected forward, elevated at 45-degrees, and combed down to the previous section. Continue cutting each section, moving up the head until you reach the natural fall.

**STEP 5**   Move to the back segment. Begin with a vertical-diagonal-back section behind the ear, with succeeding sections that become more horizontal-diagonal as the sections move up the head.

**STEP 6**   You will cross over the center back division line. This is designed to leave weight in the center, while building weight as you move up the head shape.

In the back segment, the section is overdirected toward the front and is combed downward to the previous section. Continue to cut well above the occipital bone.

**STEP 7**   Repeat procedure and methods on the opposite side of the head. Drop in the crown area and gently comb to natural growth pattern. Cut into the shape at its natural position. Use a stationary guide at the round of the head.

**CROSS CHECKING**   Cross check the back segment using horizontal-diagonal-back section. Check the technique using vertical-diagonal-back sections.

**BLOW DRY**   **A.** Flat wrap hair by blow drying hair forward and backward to remove 80% of the moisture.

**B.** After most of the moisture has been removed use a leafing technique with the same sectioning used for the cut. These methods are intended to control hair and prepare it for refinement.

**REFINEMENT**   After the blow dry phase, visually check the haircut and refine the shape, customizing it to fit your guest's needs. Finish the service by completing the style, applying PAUL MITCHELL product, and using the 2-Minute Plan.

# Round Graduation Exercise

 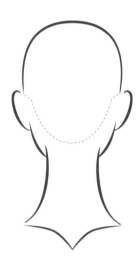 

**Notes:** _____

_____

 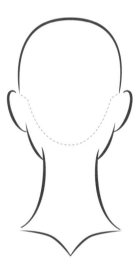 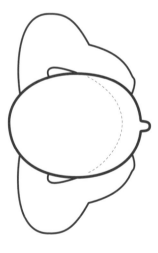

**Notes:** _____

_____

# Round Graduation Key Points

## CREATING THE BASIC SHAPE

- Create four standard segments with a natural part.
- Start in the front.
- Section the hair using horizontal-diagonal-back sections.
- Cut the hair sections using a 45-degree elevation.
- Stand in a position that is consistent with round geometry.
- Overdirect the hair slightly forward and onto the previously cut section.
- Continue to cut the hair until you reach the natural fall.
- At the sides, cut the hair using vertical-diagonal-back sections, behind the ear.
- The sections become horizontal-diagonal-back as you continue to cut the hair moving up the head shape.
- Cut the hair at a 45-degree angle and parallel to the section.
- The cutting sections will cross over the back division line.
- Continue until you reach the natural fall.
- Always use section angle accuracy.

## CROSS CHECKING

- To cross check the basic shape use vertical-diagonal-back sections.

## BLOW DRY

- **Flat wrap** – Blow dry the hair forward and backward to remove 80% of the moisture.
- **Leafing** - Blow dry the hair using the same sections used to create the basic shape.

## REFINEMENT

- Visually check the haircut and refine the shape.
- Finish the service by applying PAUL MITCHELL finishing products.
- Complete the service using the 2-Minute Plan. Recommend the appropriate PAUL MITCHELL products.

*See Product Recipe Cards for product ideas.*

# Notes

"Vee"

Round Layers

 *Round Layers*

## Haircut Description

The Round Layers haircut is cut in a convex manner around the head shape, reducing bulk, producing movement and interior texture.

## FACTORS THAT AFFECT THE HAIRCUT

| | |
|---|---|
| GEOMETRY | Round |
| TECHNIQUE | Layered |
| ELEVATION | 90-degrees |
| OVERDIRECTION | Forward |
| TENSION | Maximum |
| SECTION ANGLE ACCURACY | Vertical |
| HAND POSITION | Overhand |
| UPPER BODY | Vertical |
| LOWER BODY | Round |

## The Round Layers Exercise

### Creating the Basic Shape

**STEP 1**   Create standard segments, with center part.

**STEP 2**   Begin in the front segments with a vertical section from the apex to the front hairline in a wagon wheel pattern. Each succeeding section radiates from the apex.

**STEP 3**   Elevate sections at 90-degrees from the round of the head, parallel to the structure of the skull.

Continue taking wagon wheel sections as you progress around the head. Overdirect each section forward to the previous section. When cutting left-handed, start on opposite segment. (*See diagram.*)

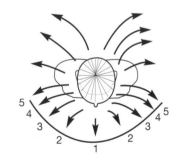

**STEP 4**     Moving into the back segments, continue to use wagon wheel sections from the apex of the head.

Remember to overdirect consistently forward to the previous section. Maintain 90-degree elevation near the round of the head.

*Note: The round gets slightly lower on the sides and back.*

**CROSS CHECKING**     Cross check the segments using horizontal-diagonal-back sections. Elevate and overdirect sections, using the same method described in creating the basic shape.

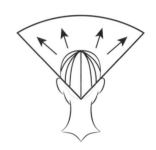

**BLOW DRY**     **A.** Flat wrap hair by blow drying hair forward and backward to remove 80% of the moisture.

**B.** After most of the moisture has been removed use a leafing technique with the same sectioning used for the cut.

**REFINEMENT**     After the blow dry phase, visually check the haircut and refine the shape, customizing it to fit your guest's needs. Finish the service by completing the style, applying PAUL MITCHELL product, and using the 2-Minute Plan.

# Round Layers Diagram

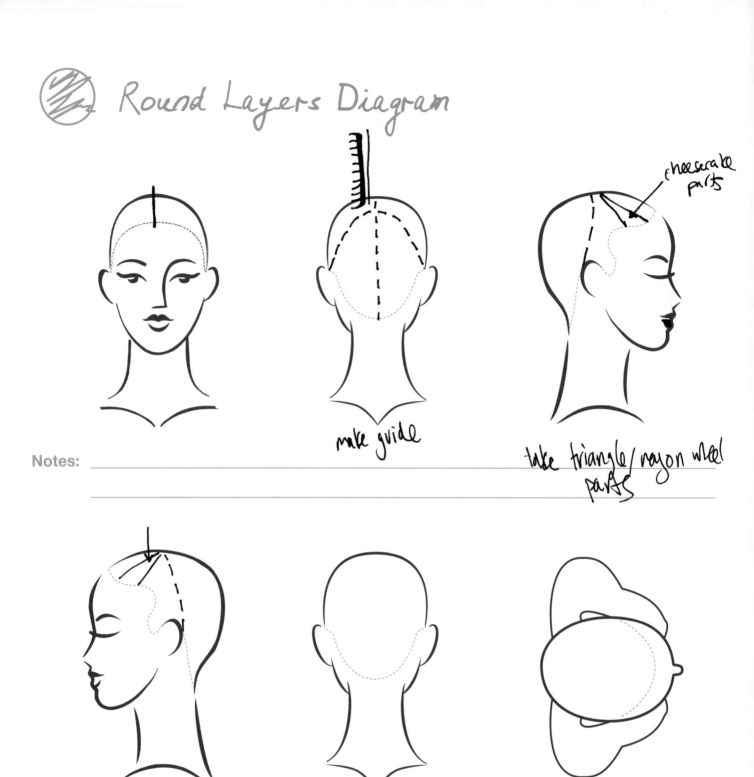

cheesecake parts

Notes: _____

make guide

take triangle/wagon wheel parts

Notes: start at apex
move towards face

make guide in each section

**PAUL MITCHELL**
**the school**

*Round Layers Key Points*

**CREATING THE BASIC SHAPE**

- Create four standard segments with a center part.
- Start the haircut in the front; take vertical sections from the apex area and working toward the front hairline.
- Elevate the hair 90-degrees from the round of the head.
- Overdirect the hair section forward onto the previously cut section.
- Use wagon wheel sectioning and continue cutting to the back.
- Stand in a position that is consistent with round geometry.
- Always use section angle accuracy.

**CROSS CHECKING**

- Cross check the basic shape back segments using horizontal-diagonal-back sections. Use the same elevation and overdirection used in creating the basic shape.

**BLOW DRY**

- *Flat wrap* – Blow dry the hair forward and backward to remove 80% of the moisture.
- *Leafing* – Blow dry the hair using the same sections used to create the basic shape.

**REFINEMENT**

- Visually check the haircut and refine the shape.
- Finish the service by applying PAUL MITCHELL finishing products.
- Complete the service using the 2-Minute Plan.
  Recommend the appropriate PAUL MITCHELL products.

*See Product Recipe Cards for product ideas.*

# Notes

Triangular One-Length

 Triangular One-Length

## Haircut Description

The Triangular One-Length shape is described as having maximum density. The haircut is cut shortest in the back and becomes gradually longer toward the face.

## FACTORS THAT AFFECT THE HAIRCUT

| | |
|---|---|
| GEOMETRY | Triangular |
| TECHNIQUE | One-Length |
| ELEVATION | None |
| OVERDIRECTION | None |
| TENSION | None |
| SECTION ANGLE ACCURACY | Horizontal-diagonal-forward |
| HAND POSITION | Cutting in comb |
| UPPER BODY | Horizontal-diagonal-forward |
| LOWER BODY | Triangular |

## The Triangular One-Length Exercise

### Creating the Basic Shape

| | |
|---|---|
| STEP 1 | Create four standard segments with a natural part. |
| STEP 2 | Start in the center back area at the nape. Use horizontal-diagonal-forward sections. Starting in the center, comb the hair to the natural fall. |
| STEP 3 | Comb hair down with the wide teeth of the comb, using no tension, overdirection, or elevation. When cutting lefthanded, start on opposite segment. |

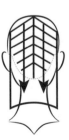

**STEP 4**   Cut from the center, working left in a normal cutting position. Continue from the center working to the right in a backhand position.

The cutting angle should be parallel to the partings. The partings should be based off the balance or angle of the jaw line.

Continue taking parallel sections up the head. Once the sections reach above the ear, sectioning should continue from the center back division line, working towards the front hairline.

When working over the ear, use the tension release method.

**CROSS CHECKING**   Cross checking a one-length shape is done by changing your scissor direction.

**BLOW DRY**   **A.** Flat wrap hair by blow drying hair forward and backward to remove 80% of the moisture.

**B.** After most of the moisture has been removed use a leafing technique with the same sectioning used for the cut. These methods are intended to control hair and prepare it for refinement.

**C.** Direct the airflow onto the end, directing the ends down and under.

**REFINEMENT**   After the blow dry phase, visually check the haircut and refine the shape, customizing it to fit your guest's needs. Finish the service by completing the style, applying PAUL MITCHELL product, and using the 2-Minute Plan.

# Triangular One-Length Diagram

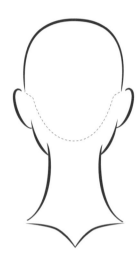

**Notes:** _____

_____

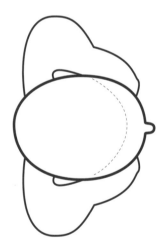

**Notes:** _____

_____

**PAUL MITCHELL**
**the school**

# Triangular One-Length Key Points

## CREATING THE BASIC SHAPE

- Create four standard segments with a natural part.
- Start at the back and center of the head.
- Use no tension or overdirection, and use 0-degree elevation.
- Use horizontal-diagonal-forward sections.
- Cut hair working from the center to the left, using a normal cutting position.
- Next, cut the hair working from the center to the right, using a backward cutting position.
- Stand in a position that is consistent with triangular geometry.
- Cut inside the comb, using the wide teeth of the comb to control the hair section.
- Use the tension release method when cutting around the ear.
- Continue to cut the hair until the natural fall is reached.
- Cut parallel to the section.
- Always use section angle accuracy.

## CROSS CHECKING

- To cross check the basic shape, change scissor direction, keeping the hair at 0-degree elevation.

## BLOW DRY

- *Flat wrap* – Blow dry the hair forward and backward to remove 80% of the moisture.
- *Leafing* – Blow dry the hair using the same sections used to create the basic shape.
- *Beveling* – Direct the airflow onto the ends, directing the ends down or under.

## REFINEMENT

- Visually check the haircut and refine the shape.
- Finish the service by applying PAUL MITCHELL finishing products.
- Complete the service using the 2-Minute Plan.
  Recommend the appropriate PAUL MITCHELL products.

*See Product Recipe Cards for product ideas.*

# Notes

PAUL MITCHELL
the school

"Myla"

Triangular Graduation

# Triangular Graduation

## Haircut Description

The Triangular Graduation haircut is described as having a buildup of weight away from the head. The hair is shortest at the nape and longest near the face.

## FACTORS THAT AFFECT THE HAIRCUT

| | |
|---|---|
| GEOMETRY | Triangular |
| TECHNIQUE | Graduated |
| ELEVATION | 1 to 89-degrees |
| OVERDIRECTION | Backward |
| TENSION | Medium |
| SECTION ANGLE ACCURACY | Vertical-diagonal-forward, pivoting to horizontal-diagonal-forward |
| HAND POSITION | Inside hand |
| UPPER BODY | Vertical-diagonal-forward, pivoting to horizontal-diagonal-forward |
| LOWER BODY | Triangular |

## The Triangular Graduation Exercise

### Creating the Basic Shape

**STEP 1**    Create four standard segments with a natural part.

**STEP 2**    Starting in the back, take a vertical-diagonal-forward section from the occipital bone, down to the hairline. Pull this section straight back about 45-degrees. Keep in mind the more or less elevation used, the heavier or lighter the graduation. Cut the section parallel to the head shape.

**STEP 3**

The next section is taken from a slightly higher point on the division line. Working slightly wider sections at the hairline, elevate and overdirect this section to the previous section.

Cut all of the subsequent sections; continue working up to the division line, while getting wider at the hairline.

Make sure the sections rotate from a vertical-diagonal-forward section to a horizontal-diagonal-forward section at the high occipital bone to the top of the ear.

Each section should be elevated and overdirected to the previous section. The rest of the sections are parallel to the section from the high occipital bone to the top of the ear and continuing from the center back division line to the front hairline. When cutting left-handed, start on the opposite segment. Work with a stationary guide at the round of the head on the top.

**STEP 4**

Working from the back toward the front, decrease elevation as you work past the ear toward the front hairline, keeping the overdirection consistent. Continue to work up the head to the natural fall. Repeat steps on the opposite side.

**CROSS CHECKING**

Use vertical-diagonal-forward sections to check graduation. Use the same elevation used during the basic shape phase. Use horizontal-diagonal-forward sections to check the geometry. Use the same overdirection as used when cutting the basic shape. Check for balance.

**BLOW DRY**

A. Flat wrap hair by blow drying hair forward and backward to remove 80% of the moisture.

B. After most of the moisture has been removed use a leafing technique with the same sectioning used for the cut.

**REFINEMENT**

After the blow dry phase, visually check the haircut and refine the shape, customizing it to fit your guest's needs. Finish the service by completing the style, applying PAUL MITCHELL product, and using the 2- Minute Plan.

# Triangular Graduation Diagram

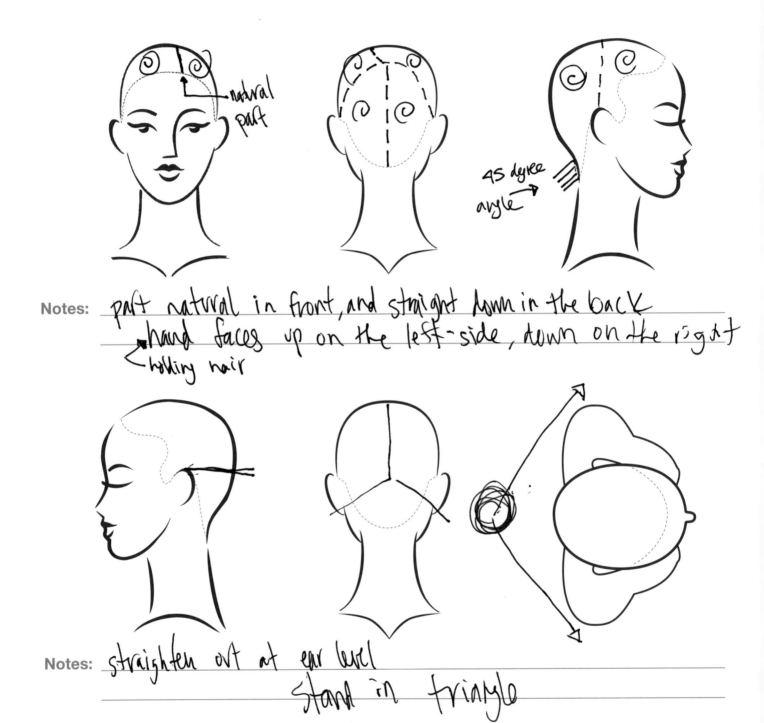

**Notes:** part natural in front, and straight down in the back
hand faces up on the left-side, down on the right
holding hair ← natural part

45 degree angle

**Notes:** straighten out at ear level
stand in triangle

**PAUL MITCHELL**
**the school**

## CREATING THE BASIC SHAPE

- Create four standard segments with a natural part.
- Start in the back.
- Section the hair using vertical-diagonal-forward sections.
- The sections will rotate from vertical-diagonal sectioning to horizontal-diagonal-forward sections.
- Cut the hair using a 45-degree elevation.
- Stand in a position that is consistent with triangular geometry.
- Overdirect the hair back onto the previously cut section.
- At the sides, from the high occipital area to the top of the ear, cut the hair parallel to the section.
- Decrease section elevation at the ear and continue to overdirect the hair back while cutting.
- Always use section angle accuracy.

## CROSS CHECKING

- To cross check the basic shape, use vertical-diagonal-forward sections.
  Use horizontal-diagonal-forward sections to check triangular geometry. Use the same section elevation that was used in creating the basic shape.

## BLOW DRY

- *Flat wrap* – Blow dry the hair forward and backward to remove 80% of the moisture.
- *Leafing* – Blow dry the hair using the same sections used to create the basic shape.

## REFINEMENT

- Visually check the haircut and refine the shape.
- Finish the service by applying PAUL MITCHELL finishing products.
- Complete the service using the 2-Minute Plan.
  Recommend the appropriate PAUL MITCHELL products.

*See Product Recipe Cards for product ideas.*

# Notes

PAUL MITCHELL.
the school

"Kate"

Triangular Layers

 *Triangular Layers*

## Haircut Description

The Triangular Layers haircut includes layers that are shortest at the back of the head and that become gradually longer toward the face.

## FACTORS THAT AFFECT THE HAIRCUT

| | |
|---|---|
| GEOMETRY | Triangular |
| TECHNIQUE | Layered |
| ELEVATION | 90-degrees |
| OVERDIRECTION | Backward |
| TENSION | Maximum |
| SECTION ANGLE ACCURACY | Vertical |
| HAND POSITION | Overhand |
| UPPER BODY | Vertical |
| LOWER BODY | Triangular |

*The Triangular Layers Exercise*

### Creating the Basic Shape

**STEP 1**   Create four standard segments, with a center part. Create a horizontal-diagonal-forward panel, from the top of the occipital bone to the top of the ears.

**STEP 2**   The first section is elevated out at 90-degrees and cut at a flat line from the floor to the ceiling, parallel to the wall.

Work from the center to the left, taking each section parallel, elevating and overdirecting to the previous section. Cut each section until you reach the ear.

**STEP 3**

The next panel is a horizontal-diagonal-forward section from the crown to the temple area at the front hairline.

Again, starting at the center division line continue cutting in the same manner as the previous panel. Continue cutting a flat line from the floor to the ceiling. Overdirect each section onto the previously cut section until you reach the ear, where the guide becomes stationary. When cutting left-handed, start on the opposite segment.

**STEP 4**

The next panel is between the crown area and apex area. Continue to use vertical sections, elevating at 90-degrees and cutting a flat line. Overdirect in the same manner as the previous panels, until you reach the division line between the apex area and the mastoid process.

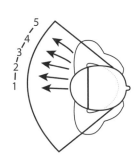

**STEP 5**

The next panel starts at the top of the head. Use horizontal sections. Overdirect the hair back to the guide cut from the previous panel at the crown area. Use a stationary guide to finish the top section.

**CROSS CHECKING**

Cross check the back segments using horizontal-diagonal-forward sections. Elevate and overdirect sections, using the same method described in creating the basic shape.

**BLOW DRY**

**A.** Flat wrap hair by blow drying hair forward and backward to remove 80% of the moisture.

**B.** After most of the moisture has been removed use a leafing technique with the same sectioning used for the cut.

**REFINEMENT**

After the blow dry phase, visually check the haircut and refine the shape, adjusting the design and customizing it to fit your guest's needs. Finish the service by completing the style, applying PAUL MITCHELL product, and using the 2-Minute Plan.

*Triangular Layers Diagram*

 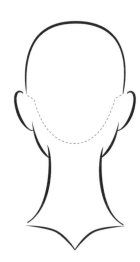 

Notes: _____

_____

 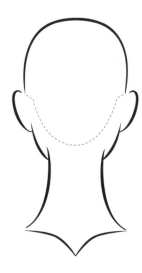 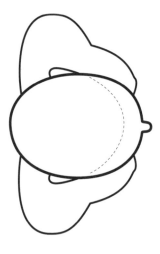

Notes: _____

_____

**PAUL MITCHELL.**
**the school**